21st Century Skills Library

GLOBAL PERSPECTIVES

IMMIGRATION

WE ALL HAVE A DREAM

Robert Green

Cherry Lake Publishing
Ann Arbor, Michigan

Published in the United States of America by Cherry Lake Publishing
Ann Arbor, Michigan
www.cherrylakepublishing.com

Content Adviser: Dr. Rita Simon, University Professor for the School of Public Affairs, American University, Washington, DC

Photo Credits: Cover and page 1, © Ted Soqui/Corbis; page 4, © iStockphoto.com/LyaC; page 6, © iofoto, used under license from Shutterstock, Inc.; page 7, © POPPERFOTO/ Alamy; page 9, © Jenny Matthews/Alamy; page 11, © Ladi Kirn/Alamy; page 13, © Peter Jordan/Alamy; page 15, © Stock Connection Blue/Alamy; page 16, © Jim West/Alamy; pages 18 and 20, © Janine Wiedel Photolibrary/Alamy; page 23, © EuroStyle Graphics/ Alamy; page 25, © Ulrich Doering/Alamy; page 26, © mediacolor's/Alamy

Map by XNR Productions Inc.

Library of Congress Cataloging-in-Publication Data
Green, Robert, 1969–
 Immigration / by Robert Green.
   p. cm.—(Global perspectives)
 Includes index.
 ISBN-13: 978-1-60279-128-2
 ISBN-10: 1-60279-128-7
 1. Emigration and immigration—Juvenile literature. 2. United
States—Emigration and immigration—Juvenile literature. I. Title. II.
Series.
 JV6035.G74 2008
 304.8—dc22   2007038853

Cherry Lake Publishing would like to acknowledge the work of
The Partnership for 21st Century Skills.
Please visit www.21stcenturyskills.org for more information.

TABLE OF CONTENTS

CHAPTER ONE
A Summit at Ellis Island   4

CHAPTER TWO
Why Do People Move?   9

CHAPTER THREE
A World of Immigrants   15

CHAPTER FOUR
The Fight over Borders   20

CHAPTER FIVE
A Global Issue   23

Map   28

Glossary   30

For More Information   31

Index   32

About the Author   32

A Summit at Ellis Island

The Ellis Island Immigration Museum is a great place to learn more about the history of immigration to the United States.

As Megan Sweeney wandered around the Ellis Island **Immigration** Center, she felt as if she were looking into her grandparents' attic, discovering bits of family history. Megan was from Ireland, but so many of her relatives had immigrated to the United States through Ellis Island that she felt familiar with it, even though she had never been there before.

In one of the rooms of the immigration center, which is now a museum, she discovered the Sweeney family name. As she looked at the records of a few of her ancestors, she could not help but feel a little choked up.

"Is that your family name?" asked a young boy named Tommy Han, introducing himself to Megan.

"Yes," said Megan, "and it makes me appreciate what my family members went through to get here."

"Tell me about it," said Tommy. "I found one of my mother's uncles' names in here, too, and I'm from Canada."

Megan looked at Tommy curiously. "But you don't look Canadian," said Megan, trying not to offend Tommy.

"Well, just what does a Canadian look like?" asked Tommy, trying to tease Megan and make a point at the same time. Because Canada, like the United States, is a nation of immigrants, it is impossible to tell if people are Canadian just by looking at them.

Megan was afraid she had offended Tommy, and she didn't know what to say.

"Oh, don't worry," said Tommy. "I get that all the time. My family is originally from China, but some members of my family moved to the United States, and others moved to Canada. Some are even still in China."

✱ ✱ ✱

Ellis Island is in New York Harbor, near the Statue of Liberty.

The United States and Canada are two nations that developed largely because people moved there from other countries. This movement of people from one country to another is known as immigration. Ellis

Island was once the first stop for many new immigrants arriving in the United States. It is on a small island in New York Harbor, across from bustling New York City, where people from all over the world rub elbows as they go about their daily lives.

From 1892 to 1954, more than 12 million immigrants came to the United States through Ellis Island. That's more people than the

An Immigrant family from Italy waits to be processed at Ellis Island in the early 1900s.

total population of countries such as Greece and Belgium. Today, about 40 percent of all Americans can trace their family history back to an immigrant who came through Ellis Island.

✳ ✳ ✳

People who are interested in immigration study the "push" and "pull" factors. A push factor is something that drives people away from their own countries. This could be governments that **suppress** individual and economic freedoms, or a lack of jobs or educational opportunities for children. Push factors also include someone's home country suffering from the effects of famine, drought, or war.

Pull factors are things that draw, or pull, people toward a new country. Common pull factors include the availability of good jobs, education, and health care. Other pull factors include freedom and the desire to reunite with family members who have already moved to a new country.

Can you think of any other push and pull factors that would influence a person's decision to leave his or her home country?

For Megan and Tommy, Ellis Island was serving another important function that day. It was the site of the International Global Issues **Summit**. Megan was a representative from Ireland, and Tommy was representing Canada. Students from all over the world were gathering on Ellis Island to investigate the subject of immigration. They wanted to find out just why so many people move from one country to live permanently in another. The **delegates** to the summit also hoped to better understand both the benefits and the problems presented by immigration.

"One thing is for certain," said Rosa Diaz, who was representing the United States at the summit, "we are all in this together. More and more people are moving all the time."

"It's almost like the whole world is on the move," said Megan.

CHAPTER TWO

WHY DO PEOPLE MOVE?

Workers bring food to children during a famine in Sudan. Famine is one factor that pushes people out of their home countries.

As the delegates to the summit settled into their chairs to discuss immigration around the world, a young man from England named James Brudenell spoke. He asked a question that was on all of their minds. "One has to wonder," said James, "just why all of these people are moving to different countries?"

When we look at why so many people are moving from one country to another, the answer lies in the search for a better life. Generally, this means more economic opportunity, such as a job or the chance to own a business. But there are other factors, too. People often move from poorer countries to richer ones, where the economy is better and more services are available. In doing so, immigrants will often endure a much harder life than they had in their own country. They do this so that their children might have access to education, health care, and other government services.

If you look at immigration on a global level, some patterns become clear. In general, people move from the **Southern Hemisphere**—places such as Africa, South America, and Southeast Asia—to the **Northern Hemisphere**. They are attracted by the individual and economic freedoms found in places such as Europe, Canada, and the United States.

Immigration patterns, however, are affected by many other factors. For example, in the Middle Eastern countries of Saudi Arabia, the United Arab Emirates, and Oman, immigrants outnumber native residents. This means that there are more immigrants than people who were born in those countries. The reason for this is that these countries are sparsely populated—they have few people—but because of the booming oil and shipping industries, many workers are needed to keep the economy running. Immigrant workers arrive from other Middle Eastern countries

An immigrant works at a construction site in Saudi Arabia. Many immigrant workers are needed to keep the country's economy running.

and from places such as India and Pakistan. These workers help keep the economies of the less-populated countries strong, while earning money through jobs that they could not find in their home countries.

When people want to enter the United States, they must apply for a **visa**. A visa grants a person from another country permission to enter the country and to stay for a certain amount of time. When the visa expires, the person must return to his or her home country. Most other countries have a similar process for people who want to enter.

A person who wants to become a U.S. citizen must go through a multistep process called naturalization. The first step is to apply for a permanent resident card, or green card. This shows that an immigrant is a permanent legal resident of the United States. The next steps include finding a steady job, attending citizenship classes, and learning English. After passing the citizenship test, immigrants take an oath of loyalty to the United States. Then they can proudly call themselves naturalized U.S. citizens.

This is an example of how legal immigration can help a country's economy. Examples like this one occur in other countries in the world, including the United States and Canada.

* * *

Rosa Diaz, the American host for the conference, jumped into the conversation. "That's exactly how my family came to the United States," she said. "My parents came from Mexico and work in Southern California. Many Mexicans move to the United States to find work."

Rosa was correct. The U.S. economy relies on a steady supply of labor. Immigrants in search of jobs often fill a shortage of workers for a particular type of job or industry.

"There is so much movement of people in the world today," said James, "that it almost seems like the world has no borders."

CHAPTER THREE

A WORLD OF IMMIGRANTS

A Guatemalan immigrant harvests basil on a farm in Florida.

A boy named Idrissa Diouf, from the West African nation of Senegal, scratched his head. He was still thinking about what James had said about so many of the world's people being on the move. He was thinking of the

*A U.S. Border Patrol agent checks a vehicle at a checkpoint
near the border between the United States and Canada.*

many West African emigrants who lost their lives trying to cross the ocean
from Africa to Europe in small, unsafe boats to start new lives. Many of the
boats sank, and the immigrants drowned.

"Although there is a lot of immigration," said Idrissa, "the world's
borders in many places are very difficult to cross, especially if you are from
certain countries or if you have little education or lack job skills."

"Yes," said James, thinking of the many immigrants from all over the world in his native England. "Immigration is controversial. Government leaders debate just who should be able to immigrate and how many people should be allowed to become new citizens. This is because **sovereign** nations have the right to control their own borders."

Idrissa and James were talking about the political aspect of immigration.

✳ ✳ ✳

While there is an economic side to immigration—jobs and labor—there is also an important political aspect to immigration. Countries control immigration through government policies. A government's policy on immigration is expressed in its immigration laws.

The United States and Canada, for example, allow many immigrants into their countries each year. But they do not allow everyone to enter. They accept only a certain number of immigrants each year, so many others are not able to enter the country.

21st Century Content

When immigrants become new citizens of their adopted country, they often retain ties to family members in their former country. Immigrants who came for jobs often send some money to the family members they left behind. In some countries, this source of income is very important. The people in those countries would have difficulty buying food, clothing, and other needs if their relatives who had emigrated didn't send them money. This is another example of how immigration and the economy are tied together.

Highly educated immigrants, such as doctors, have a better chance of being allowed to move to another country.

Immigrants have a better chance of being accepted to a new country if they are well educated or have skills that are in high demand. If they are engineers, scientists, doctors, or nurses, they will usually find it easier to immigrate to a new country.

This policy highlights the importance of economic factors in immigration. Highly educated and skilled workers are in greater demand. Workers with few skills and a poor education are in much less demand, yet there are many more of them.

✳ ✳ ✳

"Many Africans enter Europe to find jobs, even if they have to do it illegally," said Idrissa.

"The same thing happens in the United States," said Rosa. "Many Mexicans who can't get permission to immigrate or to work in the United States cross the border illegally to work."

"This is the power of opportunity," said James. "People will risk a lot to find a job and make a better life, even if it means risking arrest in a foreign country."

"So, you see," said Idrissa, "it's true that there are many people immigrating all over the world, but crossing national borders is still very difficult for most immigrants. I think it would be better if we could all just move anywhere in the world we wanted to move."

CHAPTER FOUR

THE FIGHT OVER BORDERS

*People who immigrate to France are required
to learn how to speak French.*

"I agree," said Megan. "Now that Ireland's economy is improving so steadily, some Irish people who immigrated to the United States are returning to Ireland. Why can't we just move to where the jobs are?"

"Exactly," said Idrissa, "this way we would be global citizens instead of citizens of a particular country."

"Hold on," said James. "This plan might help the economic situation, but what would happen to the **culture** of a country if so many different people moved in?"

James had touched on an important part of the immigration debate. Culture refers to the language and **traditions** of a particular group of people.

* * *

Most people are proud of the countries they call home. They want to preserve their cultural traditions. For example, the French require immigrants to learn the French language and culture. In French public schools, a Muslim, or a follower of **Islam**, may not wear traditional Muslim clothing, such as a headscarf. This is because the French do not want France to begin to look like a Muslim country. They want to preserve the "Frenchness" of France.

Some people believe that the languages and customs of immigrants enrich the culture of their country. Others believe that because immigrants change the culture of a country, they need to actively work to retain their own culture. Just as the French don't want to lose the parts of their culture and traditions that make them French, Americans don't

want to lose the things that make them uniquely American.

The effects of immigration on culture help shape government policy on immigration. People vote for politicians whose views on the issue reflect their own. Cultural factors will continue to play a strong role in immigration debates.

Despite the worries about immigration, in general it is increasing. In Europe, citizens of countries that belong to the European Union—a group of nations that cooperate on various issues—can move freely among member countries. Workers from places such as Poland, where there are many young people searching for work, move to countries that have jobs but not enough workers. Today, Poles work in Ireland, the United Kingdom, and the Netherlands. European workers are allowed to move to wherever they can find jobs.

CHAPTER FIVE

A GLOBAL ISSUE

Immigrants participate in a rally in Los Angeles in 2006.
Many people have strong opinions about immigration.

"There is another way to look at it, too," said James. "If we realize that immigration is a global phenomenon that affects all of us, we can find ways to ease the pressures to emigrate."

"We hear that a lot in the debate over Mexican immigration into the United States," said Rosa. "If Mexico's economy improved, fewer people would want to cross the border into the United States."

* * *

People usually immigrate to find work and to live in a country that offers individual freedom and better education and health care for their children. Because immigration is taking place all over the world, there have been some interesting experiments to reduce the economic incentives to immigrate.

For example, immigration is tied to global trade policies. When countries buy and sell goods, their economies are affected. By making trade and other types of economic activity easier between different countries, poor countries may become more prosperous.

The North American Free Trade Agreement (NAFTA) is one example of a trade policy that was supposed to help reduce the need for immigration from Mexico to the United States. NAFTA was supposed to make it easier for businesses from the United States and Canada to relocate to Mexico. Then Mexicans could remain at home and still find jobs that pay a good wage.

NAFTA has not been completely successful, but some people have benefited. The trade agreement reflects both the complexity of the global economy and the important relationships among international trade, employment, and immigration. Practical solutions to trade issues are still being developed.

In Africa, for example, there is a lot of farming. The fruits and vegetables grown by African farmers would bring in a lot of money if sold on the international market. But many developed countries, such as the United States and some countries in Europe, protect their farm industries from competition. This is popular in developed countries, especially among farmers, but can be viewed as unfair in a global trading environment. If African crops could be sold for higher prices, perhaps

A farmer sells bananas at a market in Tanzania. Some developed countries have trade policies that don't allow African farm products to be imported and sold.

A passport is a legal document that proves a person's identity and nationality. It is needed when traveling from one country to another.

fewer Africans would have to move to other countries in search of jobs. The relationship between trade policy and immigration shows, once again, how tightly connected the different parts of our world can be.

✳ ✳ ✳

"Some countries allow workers to come into the country temporarily," said Rosa. "This can help both the migrant workers and the country where they work."

"Yes," said Idrissa, "and when the workers go back home, they can invest some of the money they earned in their own economies. It might help avoid the need for permanent immigration."

"I agree," said James. "Immigration, of course, will continue. But we must find ways to make it benefit both the immigrant and the host country. This way, people will not worry so much about illegal immigration and learning the ways of an unfamiliar culture."

"One thing is for certain," said Megan. She was still marveling at the Ellis Island immigration room through which so many of her ancestors had passed on their way to becoming citizens of the United States. "People will always want good jobs and better lives for their families, so we had better work together to find a solution."

Learning & Innovation Skills

If you look at your bank's ATM, do you see other languages written on it? Banks offer services in other languages to help travelers and to help immigrants use the machines more easily. In many countries, there is a lively debate over whether the government should offer services in many different languages, or if everyone should speak the main language of their adopted country. Some countries, such as Switzerland, have more than one national language. Others have only one. The United States has no official language, though English is used in government offices and schools. Some people think that the United States should make English its official language. Do you think this is a good idea? If English becomes the official language, should the government still provide information in other languages to people who don't speak English?

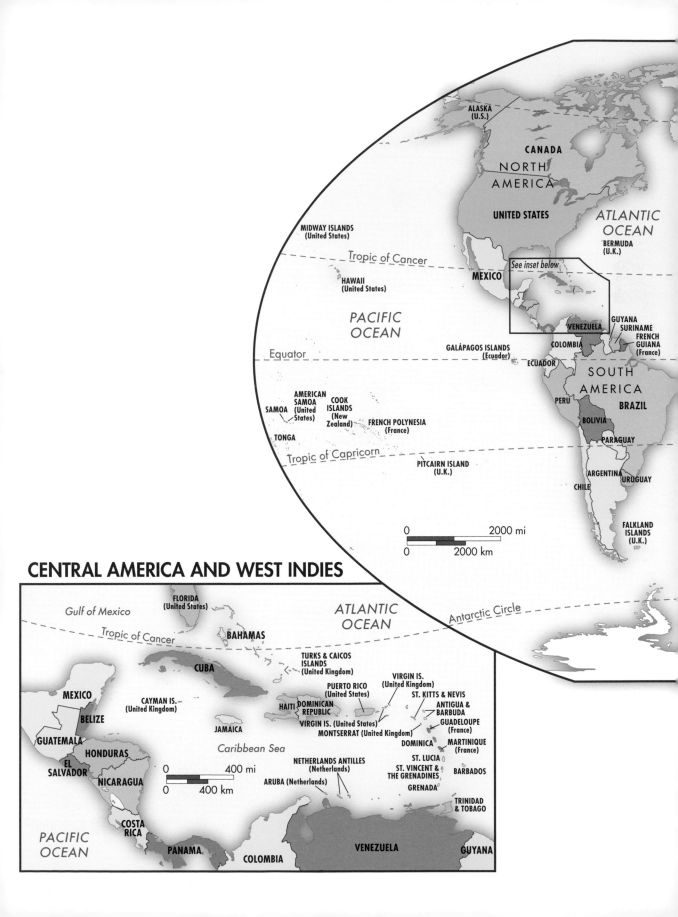

ALASKA
(U.S.)

CANADA

NORTH
AMERICA

UNITED STATES

ATLANTIC
OCEAN

MIDWAY ISLANDS
(United States)

BERMUDA
(U.K.)

Tropic of Cancer

See inset below

MEXICO

HAWAII
(United States)

PACIFIC
OCEAN

GALÁPAGOS ISLANDS
(Ecuador)

VENEZUELA

GUYANA
SURINAME
FRENCH
GUIANA
(France)

COLOMBIA

ECUADOR

Equator

SOUTH
AMERICA

PERU

BRAZIL

AMERICAN
SAMOA
(United
States)

COOK
ISLANDS
(New
Zealand)

SAMOA

FRENCH POLYNESIA
(France)

BOLIVIA

PARAGUAY

TONGA

Tropic of Capricorn

PITCAIRN ISLAND
(U.K.)

ARGENTINA

URUGUAY

CHILE

0   2000 mi
0   2000 km

FALKLAND
ISLANDS
(U.K.)

CENTRAL AMERICA AND WEST INDIES

FLORIDA
(United States)

ATLANTIC
OCEAN

Antarctic Circle

Gulf of Mexico

Tropic of Cancer

BAHAMAS

CUBA

TURKS & CAICOS
ISLANDS
(United Kingdom)

MEXICO

CAYMAN IS.
(United Kingdom)

PUERTO RICO
(United States)

VIRGIN IS.
(United Kingdom)

BELIZE

HAITI

DOMINICAN
REPUBLIC

ST. KITTS & NEVIS

ANTIGUA &
BARBUDA

GUATEMALA

JAMAICA

Caribbean Sea

VIRGIN IS. (United States)

MONTSERRAT (United Kingdom)

GUADELOUPE
(France)

DOMINICA

MARTINIQUE
(France)

HONDURAS

EL
SALVADOR

NICARAGUA

0   400 mi
0   400 km

NETHERLANDS ANTILLES
(Netherlands)

ST. LUCIA

ST. VINCENT &
THE GRENADINES

BARBADOS

ARUBA (Netherlands)

GRENADA

PACIFIC
OCEAN

COSTA
RICA

PANAMA

COLOMBIA

VENEZUELA

TRINIDAD
& TOBAGO

GUYANA

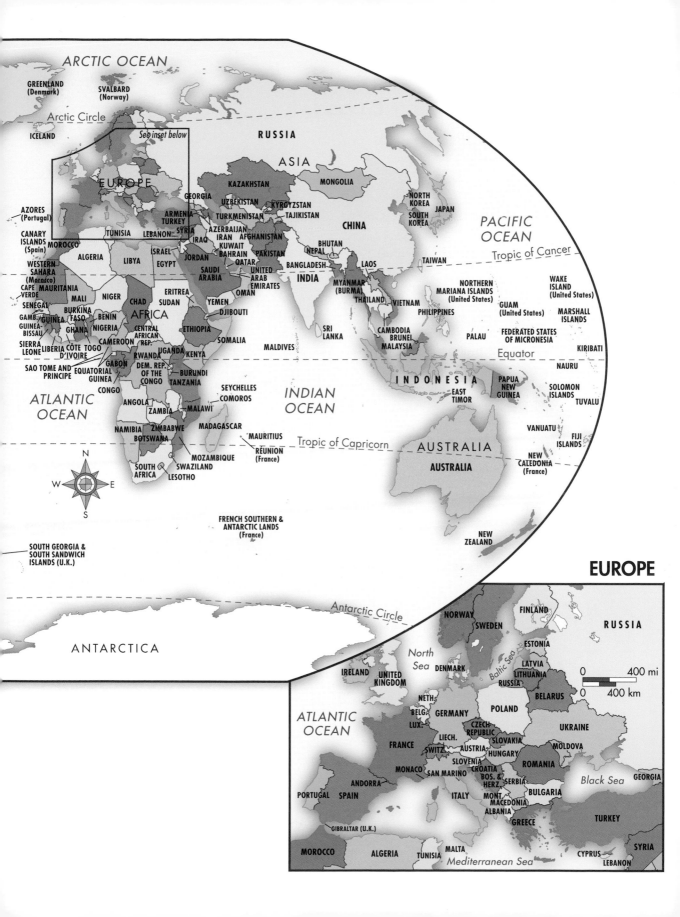

GLOSSARY

culture (KUHL-chur) the unique characteristics of a group of people, such as their customs and traditions

delegates (DEL-uh-guhts) people who represent a larger group or country at a meeting

immigration (im-uh-GRAY-shuhn) the movement of people from one country into another country

Islam (ih-SLAHM) a religion started in the Middle East that is followed by Muslims

migrants (MYE-gruhnts) people who move from one place to another to resettle or to work

Northern Hemisphere (NOR-thurn HEM-uhss-fihr) the half of the globe that lies above the equator, the dividing line that bisects Earth horizontally

settlers (SET-uhl-uhrz) people who move to a new country or area to live permanently

Southern Hemisphere (SUH-thurn HEM-uhss-fihr) the half of the globe that falls below the equator, the dividing line that bisects Earth horizontally

sovereign (SOV-ruhn) independent; having the power to control

summit (SUHM-it) a meeting of high-level leaders from different nations that addresses an international concern

suppress (suh-PRESS) to put down or control by force

traditions (truh-DISH-uhnz) cultural practices passed down from one generation to the next

visa (VEE-zuh) a document that gives permission for someone from one country to enter another country for a certain length of time

FOR MORE INFORMATION

Books

Ambrosek, Renee. *America Debates United States Policy on Immigration*. New York: Rosen Publishing Group, 2007.

Jango-Cohen, Judith. *Ellis Island*. New York: Children's Press, 2005.

Teichmann, Iris. *Immigration and the Law*. North Mankato, MN: Smart Apple Media, 2006.

Web Sites

Ellis Island
www.nps.gov/elis
Learn about the history of Ellis Island

Immigration: The Changing Face of America
memory.loc.gov/learn/features/immig/immigration_set1.html
Read about the history of immigration in the United States

National Geographic: The Genographic Project
www3.nationalgeographic.com/genographic/atlas.html
Discover the history of human movement on Earth through this interactive Web site put together by National Geographic

INDEX

Africa, 12, 15, 16, 19, 25–26

borders, 14, 16, 17, 19, 24

Canada, 5, 6, 8, 10, 12, 14, 17, 24
China, 5, 10
citizenship, 14
culture, 21, 22, 27

developed countries, 25

economies, 12–14, 17, 19, 20, 24, 25, 27
education, 8, 12, 16, 18, 19, 22, 24
Ellis Island, 4–5, 6–7, 8, 27
emigrants, 10, 16, 17, 23
England, 10, 22
Europe, 12, 16, 19, 22, 25

family, 4, 5, 7, 8, 14, 17
France, 21
freedom, 8, 10, 12, 24

governments, 8, 17, 22, 27
green cards, 14

health care, 8, 12, 22, 24

illegal aliens, 10, 19, 22
immigration patterns, 12
India, 13
Ireland, 4, 8, 20, 22
Islamic religion, 21

jobs, 8, 10–11, 12–13, 14, 16, 17, 18, 19, 20, 22, 24, 26, 27

languages, 21, 27

Mexico, 10, 14, 19, 24
Middle East, 12–13
migrants, 10, 26
Muslims, 21

naturalization, 14
Netherlands, 22
North American Free Trade Agreement (NAFTA), 24–25
Northern Hemisphere, 12

Oman, 12

Pakistan, 13
permanent resident cards. See green cards.
Poland, 22
pull factor, 8
push factor, 8

Saudi Arabia, 12
settlers, 10
Southern Hemisphere, 12
sovereign nations, 17
Switzerland, 27

taxes, 22
temporary workers, 26–27
trade, 24, 25–26

United Arab Emirates, 12
United Kingdom, 10, 22
United States, 4, 5, 6, 7, 10, 12, 14, 17, 19, 20, 21–22, 24, 25, 27

visas, 14

ABOUT THE AUTHOR

Robert Green has written more than 30 books for students. He is a regular contributor to publications on East Asia by the Economist Intelligence Unit and holds graduate degrees from New York University and Harvard University.